Historic England

Law Courts and Courtrooms 1: The Buildings of the Criminal Law

Introductions to Heritage Assets

Summary

Historic England's Introductions to Heritage Assets (IHAs) are accessible, authoritative, illustrated summaries of what we know about specific types of archaeological site, building, landscape or marine asset. Typically they deal with subjects which lack such a summary. This can either be where the literature is dauntingly voluminous, or alternatively where little has been written. Most often it is the latter, and many IHAs bring understanding of site or building types which are neglected or little understood. Many of these are what might be thought of as 'new heritage', that is they date from after the Second World War.

Criminal courts have been a key part of English life since the Middle Ages, and range from small historic, local magistrates courts to huge modern combined court centres. This document tells the story of how buildings have been adapted initially and subsequently constructed to meet the needs of England's complex criminal legal system. It also explains how the courtroom has evolved from a gathering of professionals around a table in the medieval hall to the specialised, purpose-built, modern courtroom.

This guidance note has been written by Allan Brodie and Mary Brodie and edited by Paul Stamper.

It is one is of several guidance documents that can be accessed at
HistoricEngland.org.uk/listing/selection-criteria/listing-selection/ihas-buildings/

Published by Historic England August 2016.

HistoricEngland.org.uk/listing/selection-criteria/

Front cover
Interior of Court 2 in the Sessions House at Preston, Lancashire. 1900-3, designed by Henry Littler. Listed Grade II*.

Contents

Introduction **1**

1 Criminal Law **3**

1.1 Introduction 3
1.2 The Diversity of Law Courts between the 11th and 18th centuries 3
1.3 The Buildings of the Assizes and Quarter Sessions 1700-1835 7
1.4 The Growing Complexity of plans 1835-1914 8
1.5 Assizes and Quarter Sessions Courts since 1914 10
1.6 The Changing Image of Assizes and Quarter Sessions Courts 11

2 Criminal Courtrooms **14**

2.1 The Crown Court 15
2.2 Magistrates' Courts 16
2.3 Courts of the Justice of the Peace 17
2.4 Magistrates' Courts since 1945 19

3 Criminal Courts Today **22**

4 Further Reading **24**

4.1 Contact Historic England 25

5 Acknowledgements **26**

Introduction

Although the legal system of England and Wales may be referred to as a single entity, it is in fact a series of interconnected jurisdictions with specialised practices, staff and buildings. Specific buildings have evolved during the past two hundred years to serve each of the branches, though the buildings share some common design elements, themes and symbols. Each type of courthouse contains courtrooms, offices and chambers and other rooms for judges, magistrates, coroners and other legal professionals arranged to try to guarantee an appropriate level of separation from other court users. However, courtrooms in each branch of law differ in the status of their fittings and the layout of their furniture, a reflection of the procedures in the courtroom and the character and extent of the jurisdiction of the court.

Figure 1
A conventional image of the blindfolded figure of Justice with her attributes of the scales and sword on Blackburn Magistrates Court, Lancashire. Listed Grade II.

Figure 2
'Scales of Justice' (1994) by Graham Ibbeson outside the Combined Court Centre at Middlesbrough, Cleveland. This more unconventional depiction of Justice shows a mother with her two quarrelling children.

Although different types of law court shared many features and generally followed a similar stylistic evolution, it would be difficult to confuse them. For instance, in the late 19th century Assize Courts, County Courts, Petty Sessions Courts and Coroner's Courts were all built in a Gothic style. However, each type of courthouse can be distinguished because of its location, scale and the design of the buildings. Assize Courts were among the grandest buildings in a town or city and would usually be located in the area occupied by other government buildings. Their massing would indicate that a grand public hall and large courtrooms were located within the building. Late 19th-century County Courts were often located in the commercial district of a town. Although externally they might be treated with elaborate detailing, their form would indicate that this was an office building as well as a courthouse. Magistrates' Courts were more frugal in appearance, an indication of their more humble status. Typically containing a single court, they were frequently adjacent to a police station. Purpose-built, dedicated Coroner's Courts began to be constructed during the late 19th century, particularly in London, to provide somewhere for a coroner and a jury to inspect the dead body as part of the process of reaching a verdict about a death. Due to the sensitive nature of their work, Coroner's Courts were often located in a discreet location close to a mortuary, and often in a graveyard.

Symbols frequently adorn the exterior of purpose-built law courts and town halls that contained courtrooms. The figure of Justice holds a sword, the emblem of her power, a blindfold signifies her impartiality and her scales symbolise the task of balancing right and wrong, and good and evil. The presence of Royal Arms may also denote that a building was the venue of a law court, although they also appear on other types of government buildings (Figs 1 and 2).

This survey is complemented by one which looks at civil and coroner's courts

1 Criminal Law

1.1 Introduction

Within the court system there are two broad types of law, criminal and civil. The Crown Court, like its predecessors the Assizes and Quarter Sessions, as well as the Magistrates' Court, are primarily criminal courts. Until 1971 the Assizes and the Quarter Sessions courts sat for short sessions on a few occasions each year, the differences between them being in the extent of their jurisdiction and therefore the type of judges that presided. Assize Courts were usually presided over by one of fifty-seven High Court judges though Commissioners of Assize could be appointed when a judge was unavailable, while Recorders sat in Quarter Sessions courts. There were separate Quarter Sessions for each of the 58 administrative counties of England and Wales and there were five courts of Quarter Sessions in London. Ninety-three boroughs and the City of London also had their own Quarter Sessions courts.

By 1971 the Assizes largely dealt with treason, murder, all forms of homicide, serious violence and certain forms of arson, rape and incest. Justices normally committed all other cases to the Quarter Sessions unless they considered that the case was unusually grave or difficult or because there would be a delay in hearing the case if it went to the Quarter Sessions. The Assizes also sat as a civil court and it had the same jurisdiction and powers as the High Court in London. Civil cases were heard in the *Nisi Prius* court, which might be distinguished from a criminal courtroom by the absence of a dock.

There were three exceptions to the standard system of Assizes and Quarter Sessions in London, Liverpool and Manchester. In London the Central Criminal Court was the Assize Court for Greater London, but by 1862 it was also possible to try a crime here that had been committed elsewhere. The Central Criminal Court also served as the Quarter Sessions Court for the City of London. After the Second World War, the increase in criminal activity overwhelmed the part-time Recorders presiding over the Quarter Sessions in Liverpool and Manchester. Therefore, in 1956 Crown Courts were established in both cities. Unlike the Assizes and Quarter Sessions, these were full-time courts that sat for eleven months each year.

The Courts Act 1971 replaced the Assizes and the Quarter Sessions with the Crown Court in 1972. This transformed trial by jury and the type of buildings in which this took place. The Crown Court is a single court that sits continuously in 77 centres in England and Wales. High Court Judges preside over the more serious cases at a number of sites, but full-time Circuit Judges and Recorders, who are part-time judges, deal with most cases. Each year approximately 5 per cent of criminal offences are committed to the Crown Court, the remainder being dealt with by Magistrates' Courts. The Crown Court also deals with committals for sentencing and appeals from Magistrates' Courts.

1.2 The Diversity of Law Courts between the 11th and 18th centuries

The legal system, or more accurately systems, during the Middle Ages were complex, interconnecting and frequently overlapping. Laws were created through local custom and statute, and courts of equity could provide remedies using good judgement where precedent or statutory law might not apply or be fair. There were national legal systems provided by the Crown and the Church, while local variations to the royal system applied in tin mining districts and areas of royal forest. There were also distinct courts for the counties palatine of Chester, Lancaster and Durham. At a local level there were courts for the county, hundred, borough and manor, with jurisdictions that interconnected, and sometimes overlapped, with one of the royal or ecclesiastical courts. Although the majority of cases would have been dealt with in the local courts, the most important ones, and those involving the highest members of society, were heard in the courts that evolved from the King's Council.

The complicated nature of the legal systems and the variety of levels at which cases could be heard inevitably meant that the types of buildings that were used varied greatly. Before the 18th century, purpose-built law courts and permanent furnishings were rare. Most courts were held in a convenient building in the ownership of the person or institution who presided over the court. Therefore, royal courts were held in royal buildings, either at Westminster or in the major towns of counties where the Assizes sat. Other types of court were held in any substantial, public building with a sufficiently large hall or chamber in which to lay out furniture for the trial. By the 17th century more permanent court fittings were being provided in a few buildings and some of these survive *in situ* today.

The four main Royal courts, the Exchequer, the Common Pleas, the King's Bench and the Chancery evolved from the King's Council and were at the heart of the legal system during the Middle Ages. By the 15th century the four courts were located in and around Westminster Hall (listed Grade I), which had been built about 1097-9. A manuscript in the Inner Temple Library contains illuminations illustrating the form of the four Royal courts in about 1460. In each image the judges sit on a raised bench with the Royal arms behind them. They preside over the other participants who are seated either around a large table or stand at the lower end of the courts behind a raised partition, the bar. Remnants of this type of arrangement survive today in the Consistory Court in Chester Cathedral (listed Grade I) and in the courtroom at Knaresborough Castle (North Yorkshire; listed Grade II) and in the first-floor courtroom in the Hark to Bounty Inn in Slaidburn (Lancashire; listed Grade II).

During the Middle Ages the Common Law courts and the Court of Chancery initially followed the progress of the King around the country before settling at Westminster. The Crown also dispensed justice throughout England first through the Eyre and later the Assizes. By the 14th century a system of Assizes and Quarter Sessions had evolved, in which England was divided into six assize circuits. Two or three times a year, two judges travelled from Westminster around each circuit to hear civil cases and serious criminal ones. The Assizes were also part of the mechanism of Royal government, while the Quarter Sessions was the basis of county and borough government. Therefore, during the Middle Ages the Assizes normally sat in the county hall or another building in or around a Royal castle while the Quarter Sessions were

Figure 3
Interior of the Great Hall of the 1180s at Oakham Castle, Rutland. Within the medieval hall are the remains of early 19th-century court fittings. Listed Grade I.

Figure 4
Interior of the late 16th-century courtroom in the Guildhall at Sandwich, Kent. This is one of the earliest surviving courtrooms retaining some of its original fixtures and furnishings. Listed Grade II*.

Figure 5
Interior of the courtroom at Knaresborough Castle, North Yorkshire. This late 16th-century courtroom was used for a number of courts in the locality and is now part of the museum. Listed Grade II.

usually held in prominent civic buildings. In 1971 eleven of the sixty-one Assize Courts were still located in buildings on the site of, or adjacent to, a castle, though the courts were usually housed in buildings that had been built or substantially rebuilt during the 18th or 19th centuries. However, the Assizes still sat in the Grade I-listed Great Hall of Oakham Castle in Rutland (1180s) and a Magistrates' Court sat in a room attached to the hall until a few years ago (Fig 3).

By the 16th century the Assizes and the Quarter Sessions might be held in county or town halls, often the only buildings in a town with a room sufficiently large to house the courts. In most cases the furnishings were still portable, but Sandwich Guildhall (listed Grade II*; Fig 4), in Kent, built in 1579, is unusual because it contains a fixed, purpose-built, ground-floor courtroom. Assizes and Quarter Sessions courts were held there and the Magistrates' Court still sat in the same room in the 1970s.

County Halls were built using plans similar to those employed for town halls, but they were larger and more sophisticated, as befitted a building expected to house the Assizes. The County Hall at Derby (1657-9; listed Grade I) was originally a long, single-storied hall, with the courts sitting at either end. The hall is five bays wide, with two large doorways in the façade, one for each of the Assize judges to use to enter the hall. A variation on the theme of the single hall for a county hall was employed at the Sessions House in Northampton (1675-8; listed Grade I). It consisted of an L-shaped building, designed to accommodate two courtrooms with a public area between them. The main access to the building was by two doorways at the north-west corner. The furniture of the courts dates now from the 19th century when the courts were separated from the hall between them.

Borough Courts were important during the Middle Ages, but some survived with diminishing functions until the 1970s, their longevity guaranteeing that some of the courtrooms have survived. The Guildhall at Totnes (Devon; listed Grade I) was built about 1553 and was used for borough courts as well as Petty Sessions. Major alterations occurred in 1624 and a 17th-century date seems appropriate for the bar across the courtroom, although other fittings seem to date from the 19th century. The Magistrates' Court last sat in the Guildhall in 1974. The Borough Court at Malmesbury (Wiltshire; listed Grade II*) sat in a room in the medieval hospital of St John. It retains fittings that may belong to the late 17th century and could be contemporary with the painted Royal arms dated 1693.

Although some buildings were built to provide accommodation for a specific court, others offered a facility that was used by a variety of law enforcement bodies. The Old Court House in the courtyard of Knaresborough Castle (North Yorkshire; Fig 5) originated in the early 14th century and the courtroom was located in the upper storey of a building, which was added in about 1600. Some courtroom benches and panelling remain and a trap door leads from the dock down to the cells. The court was used by the Honour of Knaresborough, the Borough Court and the Courts Leet, as well, as being used as a Forest Court.

Borough and market courts were established to deal with problems arising in distinct economic areas and in mining districts where separate legal arrangements were also often created. This occurred in areas where free-mining customs applied, such as in Derbyshire, Mendip and the Forest of Dean, and individual royal silver mines also had their own court. Therefore, the Stannaries of Devon and Cornwall were not exceptional in the Middle Ages, though their survival into the late 19th century distinguished them from most other mining areas. The tower at Lydford (Devon) probably served as a prison and a courthouse for the Stannary and the Forest of Dartmoor. It was first mentioned in 1195, but was rebuilt during the mid-13th century. At Lostwithiel (Cornwall) there are substantial remains of the Duchy Palace, which was the venue for the stannary and county court, but it is unclear whether it sat in the Convocation Hall (a masonic lodge since 1878) or the adjacent Grade I-listed Great Hall, which has now been converted into houses.

During the Middle Ages a third of England was covered by forest and a separate Forest Law enforced by verderers applied in much of this area. While the role of the forest court has declined, the courts at Lyndhurst (Hampshire) and West Dean (Gloucestershire) still have advisory roles and represent the local population's view on development. At Lyndhurst (Hampshire) the Verderer's Court is part of the Queen's House (listed Grade II*). A verderer's hall was mentioned in 1388 and the old house was enlarged during the reign of Henry VIII. Work probably began on its reconstruction in 1635, though it may not have been completed until 1671. A large ground-floor hall contains a 17th-century dock, a large table and Royal Arms dating from 1669. The Speech House (listed Grade II) at West Dean (West Sussex) was the venue for verderers' courts and mining courts for the Forest of Dean. A datestone of 1683 is located above the west entrance to the building. By 1858 the Speech House had become an inn and it was extensively enlarged in 1861. It is now a hotel and when the courtroom is not being used by the verderers, it is a restaurant and conference room. At Slaidburn (Lancashire) in the Forest of Bowland, the Hark to Bounty Inn (listed Grade II; Fig 6) contains court fittings that may have been

Figure 6
The interior of the first-floor room with 17th-century court fittings at the Hark to Bounty Inn in Slaidburn, Lancashire. Inns and public houses were often the only building in a locality with a large enough room for a court to sit. Listed Grade II.

used as a forest court. The building dates from the early 17th and late 18th century and the court furnishings on the first floor appear to date from the 17th century.

Before the Reformation all law courts, were ultimately answerable to the monarch except for ecclesiastical courts. England was divided into two ecclesiastical provinces, which were each further divided into dioceses and archdeaconries. At each of these levels there were courts, so that in the late 1820s there were more than three hundred ecclesiastical courts. Like secular courts, the furnishings in church courts were probably temporary before the 17th century. The earliest surviving church court is the Consistory Court of 1636 in the base of the south-west tower of Chester Cathedral (Fig 7). It consists of a table with benches on three sides with the raised bench occupying the fourth side. The raised position for the judges allowed them to oversee all the participants and stamped their authority on the proceedings. Apart from Chester, there are no other complete ecclesiastical courts although items of furniture survive in some cathedrals.

1.3 The Buildings of the Assizes and Quarter Sessions 1700-1835

Until the 1970s the most common location for Assize and Quarter Sessions courts were county and town halls, the seats of local government. However, by the early 19th century buildings exclusively used as law courts had evolved. These were usually located in town or city centres, though some were built alongside new prisons at the edge of expanding towns.

Originally most courts normally sat in a main hall using temporary, movable furnishings, but during the 18th century some civic buildings began to provide separate courtrooms attached to the hall. This allowed courts to work with fewer interruptions and the room could be fitted with permanent furnishings. Beside the courtrooms judges were provided with chambers and a jury room was established. The earliest example of this new building type was the Guildhall in Worcester (1721-7; listed Grade I; Fig 8), the venue for the Assizes and the Quarter Sessions of Worcestershire as well as being used for civic and social functions. The ground floor contained

Figure 7
The Consistory Court of Chester Cathedral of 1636 is a rare survivor of a fairly complete church court and shows the central role of the table in the layout of courtrooms. The Cathedral is listed Grade I.

Figure 8
The exterior of the Guildhall in Worcester of 1721-7. As well as providing a large hall and assembly room for civic and public events, the building also contained two courts for use by the Assizes. Listed Grade I.

Figure 9
The exterior of the Assize Courts in York of 1773-7 by John Carr. Placing the courtrooms at either end of the central hall created a grand composition for this classical building constructed near the Baroque early 18th-century prison. Listed Grade I.

two courtrooms behind the hall, while on the first floor there was a large assembly room, reached by the grand stair between the courtrooms. Similar arrangements were adopted for the Shire Halls at Warwick (1754-8; listed Grade I) and Stafford (1795-8; listed Grade II*), and this plan type was still employed as late as the 1830s when the Shire Hall in Worcester was built in 1834-8.

By the early 19th century purpose-built law courts were also employing this type of plan. The Assize Courts in Devizes, in Wiltshire (1835; listed Grade II*), has a small central hall with the Grand Jury room and a room for counsel flanking it. Behind these were the two courts with rooms for the jury and the judges between them. This building did not require a large hall as the town's local government functions were undertaken at the Town Hall of 1808. A similar plan was also employed in the Shire Hall in Bodmin, Cornwall (1837-8; listed Grade II*).

An alternative to placing courtrooms behind the hall was to locate them at either end, a less compact design but one that potentially increased the grandeur of the external massing. At Nottingham (1769-72) both types of plan were considered, the linear layout being preferred in this instance because it was cheaper. Frugality was not a consideration when the Assize Courts were built in York (1773-7; listed Grade I; Fig 9). Two elaborate courtrooms flank a small central entrance hall, and like Nottingham, they were originally open to the hall.

1.4 The Growing Complexity of plans 1835-1914

During the mid-19th century a long overdue reform of local government, and of the associated judicial system, took place. The issues raised by the expansion of small towns into large industrial cities were first tackled by the Municipal Corporations Act 1835 and during the course of the subsequent decades the scale of local government grew to meet the needs of an increasingly complex urban society. In the 1830s a town corporation might consist of departments for the town clerk, the police and the borough surveyor. By 1902 they might also have departments for gas, water, streets, sewers, parks, health, baths, markets, libraries, electricity, museums, schools and finance. The Municipal Corporations Act 1835 standardised the government of corporations and regularised the system for administering justice. Recorders, who were to be barristers of at least five years standing, replaced the Mayor as the judge of the borough Quarter Sessions. The Assize system was gradually extended to reflect changes in population, with Liverpool (1835), Manchester (1858), Leeds (1864) and Birmingham (1884) all becoming Assize towns.

The growing complexity of the law, the rising status of its practitioners and the increasing scope of local government led to major changes in legal and civic buildings. The small town hall and purpose-built court that had served market and county towns like Stafford in the 18th century, and continued to suffice for small towns such as Bodmin, were unsuitable for rapidly growing industrial cities. Having been granted Assize status, Liverpool Corporation chose to combine in a single scheme a project for a concert hall for the Triennial Music Festivals with new Assize Courts. The resulting building, St George's Hall (1840-55; listed Grade I; Fig 10), included a large concert hall and two principal courts in a linear layout, ultimately following the type of plan used at York seventy years earlier. However, the need to include facilities for concert-goers and the inclusion of two further minor courts, as well as rooms for the judiciary and advocates, led to the creation of a more complex plan than existed in earlier courts. The intricacy of the internal circulation, provided by means of a narrow corridor, with locked doors at strategic points, is in marked contrast to the arrangements employed in earlier courthouses.

The plan and design of the town halls in Leeds (1853-8; listed Grade I) and Leicester (1874-6; listed Grade II*) expressed the combined needs of mid-Victorian town government and justice. At Leeds, a central public hall is at the heart of the building and grouped around it, in the four corners, are three courts and a council chamber. A series of offices, Mayor's Rooms and a Bridewell were provided along the sides of the hall. Two of the courtrooms were for the Assizes of the West Riding, while the third was the Borough Court, which retains its original fittings. In the fourth corner was the Council Chamber, which later became a Crown Court.

Figure 10
The exterior of St George's Hall in Liverpool, 1840-55, by Harvey Lonsdale Elmes. This monumental presence in the heart of Liverpool demonstrated the economic might of the rapidly growing city. Listed Grade I.

Figure 11
The former Assize courts in Manchester, 1859-64, by Alfred Waterhouse. Sadly lost due to wartime damage, this magnificent Gothic building marked a shift in the favoured style from classical forms that had previously dominated court design.

Figure 12
The Victoria Law Courts in Birmingham, 1887-91, by Aston Webb and Ingress Bell. This photograph taken by Bedford Lemere in 1891 was part of a portfolio by this celebrated photographer to mark the opening of the new law courts. Listed Grade I.

The largest and most complicated new courts of the second half of the 19th century were erected in the growing cities of Manchester and Birmingham. Manchester became an Assize town in 1858 and responded by holding a competition during the following year for the design of a new Assize court building. The winning entry was submitted by the young Alfred Waterhouse. Like most of the competition entries his scheme was broadly symmetrical, due to the need to provide two equally prominent courts with access to all the accompanying facilities (Fig 11). A third, smaller Sheriff's court was also included beside the hall.

Birmingham became an Assize town in June 1884 and a competition for the new building was announced in 1885. Alfred Waterhouse, by then a leading architect, was appointed as the consulting architect and produced a sketch plan that was to be used as the basis for the entries. Initially, the intention was to include a pair of Assize Courts but three Petty Sessions courts, a Coroner's court and a police station were soon added. The winning entry by Aston Webb and Ingress Bell had the advantage over other entries of being the most regular building on an irregular site. The first Assize was held in the new building (listed Grade I) on 30 July 1891. The Great Hall, originally exclusively for legal professionals, stretches across the building and gives access to a central corridor leading back to a small central hall. The Petty Sessions courts and the Coroner's court were immediately beside the Great Hall, while the two Assize courts were nearer the rear of the building. At the rear of the building is the very elaborate, law library (Fig 12). The first floor contains offices, a barristers' and solicitors' refreshment room and the Grand Jury room. The construction of new courthouses with complex plans was not restricted to major industrial cities. The new Shire Hall in Taunton (1855-8; listed Grade II), which was not originally used for local government, contained two courts with judges' chambers behind them. There are also rooms for witnesses, solicitors, barristers, and for custody visits.

1.5 Assizes and Quarter Sessions Courts since 1914

The outbreak of the First World War marked the end of grand projects for Assize and Quarter Sessions Courts. However, in the 1930s two small courthouses were built reviving the 18th- and early 19th-century plan of two courts behind a hall. The courthouse at Chichester, West Sussex (late 1930s) has two entrances in the main façade giving access to a hall along the front of the building. Behind the hall are the two Quarter Sessions courts that were refitted at the end of the 1960s or possibly in the early 1970s.

The years immediately after 1945 were not a time when the country's economy could afford to fund any non-essential building projects, but in 1956 the pressure on the Assizes in south Lancashire led to the establishment of Crown Courts in Liverpool and Manchester. In Manchester, with the destruction of the Assize Courts during the Second World War, all the criminal courts were sitting in the Victorian Police Courts in Minshull Street and therefore, a new building was required. The Crown Court, which was officially opened on 24 May 1961, was to be the first element of a legal complex that would also include the City Magistrates' Courts, the County Court and the Coroner's Court, but only the Magistrates' Court was built (Fig 13). Prior to a major extension of the 1980s, the Crown Court contained six courts opening from the hall.

The Crown Court at Shrewsbury was the last new Assize Court built in England. Built to serve as an Assize Court, Quarter Sessions Court, County Court and Magistrates' Court, it opened in 1967 in a single-storied brick extension to the Shire Hall. The accommodation consisted of two large courtrooms with a small amount of accompanying office space, which was probably adequate for a court that sat intermittently, but was insufficient for a modern Crown Court.

Figure 13
The exterior of the Crown Court at Manchester, 1957-61. Constructed to meet the lack of accommodation following the loss of the Assize courts during the war, this was an exceptional example in the criminal court estate of a new building in a modern style.

1.6 The Changing Image of Assizes and Quarter Sessions Courts

The form of courthouses evolved between the 18th century and the 1960s to meet the changing needs of its users. Judges gradually became more remote, leading to courthouses having a separate, secure, but modest, entrance at the rear of the building. In some buildings the public was only granted access to the public galleries of the courts, but in most buildings a main, front entrance gave all participants, apart from the judiciary, access to the building. A major historic courthouse is usually located in the relatively dense heart of a town or city and therefore in many cases there is only a single façade that can be treated with any elaboration. The form and detailing of the facade helped to establish the building's function, while symbols clarified its function.

Although classical forms were dominant in court design until the middle of the 19th century, a few courts were built in different styles. The Crown Court that was added to the Shire Hall at Lancaster (1788-98; listed Grade I) was built in a rococo Gothic style, while at Lincoln Castle (1824-8; listed Grade II) a more correct version of Gothic was employed in the Shire Hall. A neo-Norman style was employed for the Shire Hall outside the prison at Oxford (1839-41; listed Grade II; Fig 14) and this inspired the design of the former Sessions House beside the prison at Peterborough (1841-2; listed Grade II).

In the middle of the 19th century there was a more concerted change to using Gothic forms, echoing a wider shift in architectural fashion. This coincided with the growing complexity of civic and legal buildings and the potentially more elaborate and decorative qualities of Gothic seems

Figure 14
The exterior of the Grade II*-listed County Hall at Oxford, 1839-41, by John Plowman. This courthouse was constructed beside the prison, a common arrangement by the mid-19th century. As late as the 1990s, Woolwich Crown Court was built beside HMP Belmarsh so that serious offenders could be tried without having to be transported by road.

Figure 15
The exterior of the Royal Courts of Justice on the Strand in London, constructed between 1871 and 1882, G.E. Street. Although the courts have been extended considerably during the 20th century, it is still the highly distinctive Gothic facade that features regularly on news bulletins. Listed Grade I.

to echo the intricate planning requirements of the larger new courts (Fig 15). Alfred Waterhouse's Assize Courts in Manchester (1859-64) reflected the appearance of a medieval town hall in the Low Countries, while the Assize Courts in Birmingham (1886-91) is more reminiscent of an elaborate French, late-Gothic chateau. In the new Shire Hall in Taunton, Somerset (1855-8) there are two courts with hammerbeam roofs on the ground floor, lit by Perpendicular-style windows.

Gothic was not used to the exclusion of other styles. In 1888 the Guildhall in Nottingham was built in a French-Renaissance style, but its complex layout includes the same elements found in contemporary Gothic designs. At the beginning of the 20th century Preston Sessions House (1900-3; listed Grade II*) and the Central Criminal Court in London (1902-7; listed Grade II*) marked a return to classical detailing, employing versions of the current Free-Baroque style. Fig 16 Between the First World War and the abolition of the Assizes and the Quarter Sessions in 1971 the few new courts adopted the current style of large public and commercial buildings.

Figure 16
The exterior of the Sessions House at Preston, 1900-3, by Henry Littler. This is one of the grand courthouses and civic buildings of about 1900 that marked a concerted return to the use of classical forms. Listed Grade II*.

2 Criminal Courtrooms

The buildings housing the Assizes and Quarter Sessions evolved from general civic buildings to dedicated law courts with complex, highly segregated plans guaranteeing that potentially conflicting groups of users were kept apart until they met in court. A similar pattern of development also applies to the layout of the courtroom, an evolution that is directly related to changes in the procedures of criminal courts.

Before a trial began at the Assizes and Quarter Sessions, a Grand Jury of between twelve and twenty-three county freeholders was summoned to hear bills of indictment. They heard as much of the prosecution evidence as was necessary to establish whether it was sufficient to indict the accused and if so, a trial would be heard before an ordinary jury. By the 19th century the Grand Jury had a separate, dedicated room for their deliberations. Once they reached a decision, their foreman passed it to the Clerk of the Assize from a separate gallery in the courtroom. This might be done using a 'gaff', a long rod with a clip on the end to hold the 'bill'. This procedure continued until 1933 when Grand Juries were abolished.

Within the courtroom the table was at the heart of the furnishings during the Middle Ages and it remained a key feature in purpose-built, permanent courts until the 19th century. Fig 17 In early courts defendants were held at the bar across the front of the court, but by the 19th century they were normally held in a dock. The term 'dock' owes its origins to criminal slang, which appropriated the Flemish term '*dok*' or '*docke*' meaning a cage or rabbit hutch. In the early 19th century it was often a small box with panelling similar in height to the furnishings housing other court users. Since the 19th century it has grown in size and the extent of the security it provided. Docks were usually near the heart of the court, with the public being seated behind and sometimes in a gallery above. The dock's location equated to where the prisoner stood at the bar of earlier courts. Assize courts furnished as late as the 1960s, such as at Exeter and Chichester Crown Courts, still had the dock near the centre of the courtroom with public seating behind.

Figure 17
The interior of the courtroom in the former courthouse at Ripon, North Yorkshire, of about 1830. This very complete courtroom interior shows the central position of the table with the witness box and two docks to the left and the magistrates' bench to the right. Listed Grade II*.

However, by the time that Winchester Combined Court Centre opened in 1974 the docks were at the rear of the courts with a public gallery above them. In modern Crown Courts the docks are at the rear of the court, often set within structural walls to improve security. Public seating is normally towards the rear of the courtroom and in historic courts it was often located behind the dock and in a gallery above.

Juries were an essential part of major criminal trials, but until 1670 they were obliged to follow the judge's direction. They would consider their verdicts after a group of cases, each lasting only a few minutes, though by the late 17th century they were instead reaching a verdict at the end of each case. As trials were so brief, verdicts were frequently reached while still sitting in the jury box. Juries could retire to a room, but to encourage them to agree on a verdict quickly they were deprived of food, drink and any heating or light. It was only in 1831 that a majority verdict of at least nine jurors became acceptable after a deliberation of twelve hours. In large, modern, purpose-built law courts rooms for juries and judges are now usually arranged along a corridor behind the courts.

The furnishings in a medieval hall were on a single level, apart from the seating on the dais at the upper end of the hall. This distinction for the bench was adopted in the earliest permanent courtrooms and has continued until the present day. During the 19th century, probably in an effort to acknowledge its importance and dignity, the elevation of the bench above the rest of the court increased, reaching its maximum at the Central Criminal Court (opened 1907), where the benches of the original courts are between six and eight steps above the floor of the courtroom.

The *Consultative Memorandum on the Design of Courts*, published in 1971, outlined how courts would be designed in the future. At the heart of its philosophy was the need to provide a courtroom with as few levels as possible and this has been the basis of all courtroom designs since (Fig 18). It also marked the start of the creation of a new type of law court – The Crown Court.

Figure 18
The interior of Court 1 in the Combined Court Centre in Sheffield, by The Napper Collerton Partnership, 1996. This view from the bench shows a modern courtroom with a gently sloping floor to facilitate disabled access.

2.1 The Crown Court

By the 1960s the need for fundamental change was widely recognised. The Government appointed Lord Beeching in 1966 as Chairman of the Royal Commission on Assizes and Quarter Sessions, a review that took three years to complete. The report stated that the ultimate ideal was to have purpose-built court buildings in selected centres designed to a common pattern and capable of expansion. The extent of facilities provided in new Crown Courts would separate future buildings from those built for the Assizes. Although judges and juries always had separate rooms, few other users had individual facilities in older courthouses. In 1971 criminal trials by jury took place in 144 towns and cities, but the creation of the Crown Court meant an immediate decrease in the number of sites that would be needed when the Crown Court replaced the Assizes in 1972.

Although there were a number of closures, most of the buildings that were used by the Assizes and the Quarter Sessions initially continued in use. However, during the 1970s two new buildings opened with their origins in the years immediately prior to the creation of the Crown Court. In a 1967 report on spending on court building, £21 million was assigned for Assize and Quarter Sessions courts between 1964/5 and 1970/1. The new courthouse at Winchester was the largest project in the list and it was expected to cost £2.6 million, an eighth of the whole programme. This building was begun in 1966/7 and opened officially on 22 February 1974.

Although the courthouse at Winchester (and a far more modest one at Merthyr Tydfil, in Wales) contained many elements that would become essential features in new court designs, the earliest purpose-built Crown Courts designed and built after 1971, were not completed until the early 1980s. New courthouses opened at Burnley and Leicester in 1981, while those at Bolton, Chelmsford, and Portsmouth were completed in the following year. These courthouses contained between four and eight courtrooms, but in 1983 two huge combined court centres opened in Leeds and Liverpool, respectively housing 17 and 28 courts. Combined court centres contain accommodation for the Crown Court and a smaller suite of rooms for the County Court. Both share a common central entrance, but the County Court usually has a separate seating area for people waiting to see the District Judges in their chambers. The civil courtrooms differ from criminal courts in having no dock and they may have moveable, rather than fixed furnishings. During the 1980s and 1990s, 35 of the 52 new buildings provided for the Crown Court were combined court centres. Although the combined court centre is a modern building type, its dual function echoes the arrangement of the Assize Courts where both criminal and civil cases were heard (Fig 19).

Figure 19
The exterior of the Combined Court Centre in Bradford, of 1992-3. Modern court designs seek to embrace current architectural thinking and often reference courts' historical roots, such as by the use of columns evoking their classical predecessors.

In the report of the Royal Commission in 1969 a stated aim was to locate the Crown Court in a series of purpose-built modern courthouses, but some historic buildings have proved to be adaptable. The most dramatic modernisation of a 19th-century court building is the Crown Court at Minshull Street in Manchester (listed Grade II), built as the City Police Courts in 1868-71. Following the destruction of the Assize Courts in 1941 it was also used by the Assizes. In 1956 it became the home of the newly created Crown Court in Manchester and, despite the construction of a new Crown Court in 1960, it has retained this function. By the 1980s it was apparently a 'sad and unloved relic', which was 'overwhelmed by the increasing complexities of modern criminal court practice, and suffering from severe decay'. It closed in 1989 and between 1993 and 1996 it was refurbished.

2.2 Magistrates' Courts

The modern court of summary justice is the Magistrates' Court, a name that has applied since 1949. Prior to this, summary criminal courts were known as Police Courts, Petty Sessions Courts or Courts of Summary Jurisdiction. Approximately 95 per cent of all criminal cases are dealt with in the Magistrates' Court in front of two or three lay magistrates or one professional District Judge (Magistrates' Courts), formerly known as a stipendiary magistrate.

The jurisdiction of the modern Magistrates' Court and its buildings are due to the development of the role of the Justice of the Peace in local society. Since the Statute of Westminster in 1327 local worthies have been involved in the administration of the law in and around the area in which they resided. The Petty Sessions originated during the Middle Ages as a means of dealing with pressing administrative matters and minor offences between sittings of the Quarter Sessions. By the 16th century it was common for two or more Justices to meet informally every three or four weeks. Their duties included the inspection of gaols and bridges, hearing the reports of the high constables and the settling of disputes. They had powers to arrest, examine without counsel and give judgement on minor offences. The Petty Sessions soon became an established element in the administration of local government, sitting at regular times in designated locations and by the end of the 17th century they were dealing with most minor crimes and local quarrels.

The variety of buildings used in the administration of summary justice have ranged from justices' private houses and inns to purpose-built police stations containing courts, local government buildings and combined court buildings. The evolution of the Magistrates' Court building reflects the increasing formality and status of the court of the magistrate. The formation of county and borough police forces in the 19th century and the role of the police in the prosecution of offences in front of the Justices of the Peace resulted in a close association between police stations and Petty Sessions courts until the mid-20th century. However, attitudes towards how closely the police should be involved in the prosecution process changed and this was reflected in the increasing number of modern Magistrate Court buildings that have been constructed as a distinct entity, independent of a police station.

2.3 Courts of the Justice of the Peace

In 1845 a Parliamentary Return listed the locations of all the Petty Sessions sittings in England and Wales. These included private houses, inns, town halls, schools, police stations, solicitors' offices, workhouses and gaols, but the number of purpose-built law court buildings was low. At some of the Justices' private dwellings, and within public houses, there were attempts to create a more formal courtroom atmosphere. At Aberford (West Yorkshire) 'A large Room at the Rose and Crown Inn, the entrance from the public street, and fitted up purposely for the magistrates' was used. The Black Bull Inn at Birstall (listed Grade II; Fig 20), also in the West Riding, was also used by magistrates. A room on the first floor of the 17th century building contains remnants of a courtroom, including two panelled boxes. Both are decorated with symbolic paintings; one features a blindfolded figure of Justice slaying monsters with the sword

Figure 20
The interior of the first-floor, 17th-century, courtroom in the Black Bull Inn at Birstall, West Yorkshire. In the south-east corner of the room the dock survives with a painting of the figure of Justice on it. Listed Grade II.

in her right hand, while in her left she carries a set of scales. The second painting features a Druid's altar, harking back to a pre-Christian form of justice where the role of the Druid also included the functions of a lawyer and a judge.

Second in number to public houses, inns and hotels in the 1845 Return were a generic group of public buildings called town halls, guildhalls, moot halls and market halls. While the descriptions provided suggest the use of convenient rooms rather than formal courtrooms, some of the town halls did house purpose-built courtrooms. The Guildhall at Helston in Cornwall (1839; listed Grade II) contained a first-floor courtroom used for both the Petty and Quarter Sessions, as well as by the council. Dudley Town Hall was the venue for Petty Sessions for both the counties of Staffordshire and Worcestershire and the courtroom was described as:

> 'A spacious Room over the Market Hall in the centre of the town of Dudley, called the Public Office, and used only for magisterial and public meetings, fitted up with elevated desk and seats for the magistrates; desk and table for the clerks, reporters, and advocates; bar and place of confinement for persons charged with offences; witnesses and constables' boxes, and space for the public, with two adjoining Rooms for the clerks and officers in attendance.'

Town hall buildings often included judicial symbolism on the exterior to signify the presence of courtrooms. The side and front elevations of the Town Hall at Trowbridge (Wiltshire; listed Grade II) are decorated with carved stone reliefs extolling Victorian morals, two of which relate directly to its court function. One includes the scales and sword of justice with the legend '*JUSTICE*' entwined between them. The second is located over the magistrates' entrance and threateningly has a truncheon with the legend '*OBEY MAGISTRATES*' over it.

In the early 20th century the civic centre began to develop as an alternative architectural type to the town hall. It was a grouping of several buildings on one site, housing municipal administration and arts and entertainment venues. In effect, the multi-purpose town hall was split up. Where there was inadequate court accommodation in the town, law courts would also be included in civic centre schemes. Southampton Civic Centre (1928-39; Fig 21) consists of four blocks, each with their principal facade facing outwards. To the north is the public library, art gallery and art school; to the east is the guildhall and to the south are the municipal offices. At the western side is the law court block, which includes a clock tower. The law courts, which served both the borough Quarter Sessions and the Petty Sessions, opened in 1933.

Figure 21
Exterior of the Civic Centre, former Law Courts, at Southampton, opened 1933, by E. Berry Webber. By the inter-war years the administrative needs of some towns and cities prompted the creation of civic centres, sometimes including separate courthouses. Listed Grade II*.

< < Contents

Figure 22
The exterior of the former Magistrates Court in Lambeth, Greater London, 1869, by Thomas Charles Sorby. Sorby was more famous for his Italianate County Courts, but used Gothic detailing for this magistrates court as that style had become associated with criminal courts. Listed Grade II.

Figure 23
The exterior of the former Police Station and Petty Sessions Court at Tetbury, Gloucestershire, 1884, by James Medland. This is one of a group of combined police stations and magistrates' courts, constructed in Gloucestershire in stone in a Gothic style to match local buildings. Listed Grade II.

Although town halls often contained Magistrates' Courts, the Petty Sessions Court is perhaps most often found alongside or within the Police Station. While some purpose-built police and court buildings did exist prior to 1856, the second half of the 19th century saw the erection of a large number of purpose-built, combined police stations and Petty Sessions courts (Fig 22). The most comprehensive programme of 19th-century Petty Sessions court building occurred in Gloucestershire. Sixteen purpose-built, combined police stations and Petty Sessions courts were built for the county authorities in Gloucestershire between 1858 and 1909. The forms and styles of the Gloucestershire buildings echoed the existing townscapes, yet they were visually distinct enough for their function to be recognised. Two- and three-storied Tudor-gothic style buildings were the most common design and the building materials and detailing employed reflected local traditions (Fig 23).

Petty Sessions courts were also constructed alongside though separate from police stations, in one of the current architectural styles. At Burton upon Trent, Staffordshire, a two-courtroom Petty Sessions court (listed Grade II) was erected in 1909-1910 in the popular, contemporary Baroque revival style. The front elevation is faced in stone and has stone and brick returns connecting it to the police station to the rear. There are two main entrances in the front elevation, one for the '*PUBLIC*' and the other for the '*JUSTICES*'. In style Burton reflected the current taste for classical forms, but during the 1930s some combined police stations and Petty Sessions courts began to adopt modern styles, examples including Weston-super-Mare (1934; listed Grade II), Minehead (1936), Yeovil (1938) – these three in Somerset – and Northampton (1941). Accrington Police Station and Magistrates' Court, Lancashire (1933-4; listed Grade II; Fig 24), was part of a scheme that also included an adjacent fire station.

2.4 Magistrates' Courts since 1945

The Justices of the Peace Act 1949 formally ended the official use of the terms 'Petty Sessions Court' and 'Police Court' following proposals by the Departmental Committee on Justices' Clerks. Instead the title 'Magistrates' Court' was adopted. The gradual separation of Magistrates' Courts from police stations after the 1949 Act continued during

Figure 24
The exterior of the Police Station and Magistrates' Court at Accrington, Lancashire, 1933-4, by Sir Percy Edward Thomas. This courthouse was built along with a police station and fire station in a stark, stripped down classical style. Listed Grade II.

Figure 25
The exterior of the Magistrates' Court in Chesterfield, Derbyshire, 1963-5, by the practice of Professor Joseph Stanley Allen in association with R. Keenleyside. Instead of traditional forms and styles, this building boldly adopts a modern idiom in marked contrast to the nearby, inter-war town hall. Listed Grade II.

the 1950s and 1960s at locations such as Harlow (Essex, 1956), Corby (Northamptonshire, 1959), Exeter (Devon, 1960), Bracknell (Berkshire, 1964) and Peterlee (Durham, 1964). Court blocks that shared a site with a police station would be differentiated by the number of storeys, as at Corby, or their orientation, as at Exeter. Wholly independent Magistrates 'Courts were also constructed, the most spectacular being at Chesterfield (Derbyshire; Fig 25). During the 1960s a major redevelopment scheme was proposed for the centre of the town, but the only building to emerge was the new Magistrates' Court, located in Shentall Gardens below the 1937-8 town hall. The concrete-framed design was radical and unique in consisting of two fan-shaped blocks linked at their centre.

Despite the reduction in the number of Petty Sessions Areas, new Magistrates' Court buildings continued to be erected. They were designed to replace outdated accommodation in the immediate vicinity and to cope with the business that was transferred to them from older, smaller courts that were closing. New Magistrates' Courts opened during the 1990s in some of the largest cities in the country and are among the most impressive law court buildings in the justice system today.

These buildings not only replaced the old accommodation in those cities but also those in neighbouring Petty Sessions Areas. In West Yorkshire, Leeds Magistrates' Court (1988-94) replaced three court locations in the city and the courts that were previously held in the town halls of Pudsey and Morley. When it opened it was the largest purpose-built Magistrates' Court in the country with twenty-one courtrooms. Nottingham Magistrates' Court (1993-6) was built on a city-centre brown-field site of a former railway goods siding and like Leeds it replaced a variety of court locations.

Smaller towns were also provided with new courts as part of a programme of closing small, occasionally used courts and consolidation into fewer sites. In Wiltshire, Chippenham Magistrates' Court (1997; Fig 26) has a first-floor level linear layout of two formal and two informal courtrooms behind a light and airy public hall. One of the two informal courtrooms can be screened off and reached by a separate staircase to allow it to serve as a Youth Court and a Family Proceedings Court. All four courtrooms have access to the ground-floor custody suite and offices, and behind them is the magistrates' corridor, which gives access to four retiring rooms.

Figure 26
The exterior of the Magistrates' Court in Chippenham, Wiltshire, opened 1997. This modern, purpose-built magistrates' court has a main entrance designed to echo classical courthouses. It is earmarked to close in 2017.

3 Criminal Courts Today

At the beginning of the 21st century significant modernising reforms to the criminal justice system resulted from the Criminal Courts Review and the subsequent white paper *Justice for All*, which was published in July 2002. These were designed to make the criminal system work more seamlessly from initial hearings at Magistrates' Courts all the way up to the Court of Appeal and the House of Lords. In place of the Lords, the United Kingdom Supreme Court was established in 2009 in Middlesex Guildhall (1906-15). The White paper also recommended that some urban courts should sit during evenings, nights and at weekends and that the programme of improving court accommodation should continue. It was envisaged that new purpose-built facilities might include accommodation for criminal and civil courts as more combined court centres were constructed. Replacing hundreds of sites with fewer modern ones would allow the developing information technology to be incorporated more effectively, and from March 2002 every prison handling remand prisoners had a video link to a Magistrates' Court.

Although savings through modernisation and efficiencies were part of the objective of these reforms, the need to retain the link between local communities and the justice process was not to be overlooked. To do this Local Justice Boards were established bringing together in partnership the chief officers from each of the core Criminal Justice Agencies, with responsibility for overseeing and delivering criminal justice services across a police force area. These boards were originally set up in all 43 Force areas by central government and received funding, but now operate as a voluntary partnership in most counties in England.

The reforms of criminal and civil courts include an emphasis on improving access to courts and the justice system. The Disability Discrimination Act of 1995 prompted the Court Service to ask the Royal Association for Disability and Rehabilitation (RADAR) to review the access to courts for disabled people. The existing estate was examined and an implementation strategy developed to meet the requirements of the Act by 2005. Inevitably smaller, older court locations proved more complex and more expensive to adapt to modern access requirements and new IT and therefore inevitably many of these have closed during the past decade.

In 2016 HM Courts and Tribunal Service, which was established in 2011, confirmed a major round of courts closures, 86 of the 460 courts and tribunal hearing centres, being earmarked to shut by 2017. This program is expected to yield savings to the £500m annual cost of the courts estate, but will inevitably lead to justice being geographically further away from some of the public. Among the closures are the Combined Court Centre at Chichester and the two Crown Courts at Barnstaple (Devon) and Dorchester (Dorset). Two Combined Crown Courts and Magistrates Courts, and a dozen combined Magistrates Courts and County Courts will also close, along with 42 Magistrates Courts, 17 County Courts and around a dozen tribunal, office and miscellaneous legal centres.

4 Further Reading

There are many general books on the history of the law or parts of it, ranging from books on the assizes and the mediaeval county court to works about modern branches of the law. For instance, James Cockburn wrote *A History of English Assizes 1558-1714* (1972) and in the same year Sir Basil Nield penned his *Farewell to the Assizes* (1972), a lament for a system that was replaced in that year by the Crown Court. Robert Palmer published a study of *The County Courts of Medieval England 1150-1350* (1982) and more recently Patrick Polden has published *A History of the County Court, 1846-1971* (1999), a detailed study of the modern County Court. A different angle on the law is to look at the practitioners and Esther Moir published *The Justice of the Peace* (1969) as well as a detailed examination of the work of Justices of the Peace in Gloucestershire during the late 18th century.

While books on the history of the law may be plentiful, fewer address the buildings in which the law was practised. Clare Graham completed her doctoral thesis *The Development of the Law Court as a Building Type in England Before 1914* at the University of Sheffield (1997) and used it as the basis for her book *Ordering Law: The Architectural and Social History of the English Law Court* (2003). Following a national survey of prisons, *English Prisons an Architectural History* (2001), English Heritage also produced a report for the Court Service, entitled *The Law Court 1800-2000: Developments in Form and Function* (2002). This study is available in the Historic England library in Swindon.

As one of the largest and most prestigious buildings in any town, law courts often figure prominently in local histories and are particularly well documented in the volumes of the Victoria County History. The history of courts and their buildings are also described in major works of architectural history such as Howard Colvin's landmark *The History of the King's Works* (1963-82) and Christopher Chalkin's *English Counties and Public Building 1650-1830* (1998). Courts also feature prominently in other works on public buildings such as Colin Cunningham's book on *Victorian and Edwardian Town Halls* (1981). The same author also published with Prudence Waterhouse a book on the work of the leading Victorian architect *Alfred Waterhouse 1830-1905* (1992), while David Brownlee published *The Law Courts The Architecture of George Edmund Street* (1984).

4.1 Contact Historic England

East Midlands
2nd Floor, Windsor House
Cliftonville
Northampton NN1 5BE
Tel: 01604 735460
Email: eastmidlands@HistoricEngland.org.uk

East of England
Brooklands
24 Brooklands Avenue
Cambridge CB2 8BU
Tel: 01223 582749
Email: eastofengland@HistoricEngland.org.uk

Fort Cumberland
Fort Cumberland Road
Eastney
Portsmouth PO4 9LD
Tel: 023 9285 6704
Email: fort.cumberland@HistoricEngland.org.uk

London
1 Waterhouse Square
138-142 Holborn
London EC1N 2ST
Tel: 020 7973 3700
Email: london@HistoricEngland.org.uk

North East
Bessie Surtees House
41-44 Sandhill
Newcastle Upon Tyne
NE1 3JF
Tel: 0191 269 1255
Email: northeast@HistoricEngland.org.uk

North West
3rd Floor, Canada House
3 Chepstow Street
Manchester M1 5FW
Tel: 0161 242 1416
Email: northwest@HistoricEngland.org.uk

South East
Eastgate Court
195-205 High Street
Guildford GU1 3EH
Tel: 01483 252020
Email: southeast@HistoricEngland.org.uk

South West
29 Queen Square
Bristol BS1 4ND
Tel: 0117 975 1308
Email: southwest@HistoricEngland.org.uk

Swindon
The Engine House
Fire Fly Avenue
Swindon SN2 2EH
Tel: 01793 445050
Email: swindon@HistoricEngland.org.uk

West Midlands
The Axis
10 Holliday Street
Birmingham B1 1TG
Tel: 0121 625 6870
Email: westmidlands@HistoricEngland.org.uk

Yorkshire
37 Tanner Row
York YO1 6WP
Tel: 01904 601948
Email: yorkshire@HistoricEngland.org.uk

5 Acknowledgements

Images
© Historic England
Front cover: AA006995

Figure 1: AA006906

Figure 2: AA012665

Figure 3: BB013531

Figure 4: BB91_21349

Figure 5: DP033550

Figure 6: AA028536

Figure 7: CC66_00810

Figure 8: AA66_05906

Figure 9: DP072414

Figure 10: AA98_04349

Figure 11: AA012977

Figure 12: BB11058

Figure 13: AA011338

Figure 14: BB96_10594

Figure 15: DD97_00522

Figure 16: AA006979

Figure 17: AA006720

Figure 18: AA012742

Figure 19: AA012726

Figure 20: AA028864

Figure 21: AA017118

Figure 22: AA034832

Figure 23: AA008859

Figure 24: AA006900

Figure 25: AA006775

Figure 26: AA009646

Every effort has been made to trace the copyright holders and we apologise in advance for any unintentional omissions, which we would be pleased to correct in any subsequent editions.

Historic England

We are the public body that looks after England's historic environment. We champion historic places, helping people understand, value and care for them.

Please contact
guidance@HistoricEngland.org.uk
with any questions about this document.

HistoricEngland.org.uk

If you would like this document in a different format, please contact our customer services department on:

Tel: 0370 333 0607
Fax: 01793 414926
Textphone: 0800 015 0174
Email: customers@HistoricEngland.org.uk

All information and weblinks accurate at the time of publication.

Please consider the environment before printing this document

HEAG140
Publication date: August 2016
Design: Historic England

Printed in Dunstable, United Kingdom

91218508R00018